GREEK GODS UNDER QUARANTINE

A one-act comedy by
Dean O'Carroll

www.youthplays.com
info@youthplays.com
424-703-5315

 ISBN 978-1-62088-962-6.

COPYRIGHT RULES TO REMEMBER

1. To produce this play, you must receive prior written permission from YouthPLAYS and pay the required royalty.

2. You must pay a royalty each time the play is performed in the presence of audience members outside of the cast and crew. Royalties are due whether or not admission is charged, whether or not the play is presented for profit, for charity or for educational purposes, or whether or not anyone associated with the production is being paid.

3. No changes, including cuts or additions, are permitted to the script without written prior permission from YouthPLAYS.

4. Do not copy this book or any part of it without written permission from YouthPLAYS.

5. Credit to the author and YouthPLAYS is required on all programs and other promotional items associated with this play's performance.

When you pay royalties, you are recognizing the hard work that went into creating the play and making a statement that a play is something of value. We think this is important, and we hope that everyone will do the right thing, thus allowing playwrights to generate income and continue to create wonderful new works for the stage.

Plays are owned by the playwrights who wrote them. Violating a playwright's copyright is a very serious matter and violates both United States and international copyright law. Infringement is punishable by actual damages and attorneys' fees, statutory damages of up to $150,000 per incident, and even possible criminal sanctions. **Infringement is theft. Don't do it.**

Have a question about copyright? Please contact us by email at info@youthplays.com or by phone at 424-703-5315. When in doubt, please ask.

CAST OF CHARACTERS

ZEUS, king of the gods. God of thunder and lightning.

HERA, queen of the gods. Goddess of marriage.

ARES, god of war.

APHRODITE, goddess of beauty and love.

EROS, god of love.

ATHENA, goddess of wisdom and war.

THE SPHINX, a cat-like monster, female.

DIONYSUS, god of wine and theatre.

HERMES, god of messengers and thieves.

APOLLO, god of the sun, poetry, and music.

HEPHAESTUS, god of blacksmiths.

POSEIDON, god of the ocean.

HESTIA, goddess of the hearth.

ARTEMIS, goddess of the moon and the hunt.

HERCULES, god of strength.

ARACHNE, formerly a human weaver, turned into a spider, female.

DEMETER, goddess of grain.

PERSEPHONE, goddess of spring.

HADES, god of the Underworld.

PANDORA, a woman by the gods thousands of years ago.

Double-casting and gender-blind casting are highly encouraged. Characters could be doubled with any character they don't need to interact with.

ACKNOWLEDGMENT

Greek Gods Under Quarantine was first produced by Sacred Heart Middle School in Atherton, CA on October 23-24, 2020 with the following production team and cast:

Director, Rachel Prouty; Technical Director, Fred Eiras; Publicity, Betsy Burdick; Hair/Makeup Consultant, Lindsay Saier; Costumes, Mae Matos and Lisa Rozman; Sound Design/Webinar Host, Forrest Jensen; Stage Manager, Hayley Roberts; Hair & Makeup, Ava O'Donnell-Fernando; Set Design Assistants, Esan Khan and Katherine Wolf; Publications Assistant, Allison Min; Sound Operator, Dominic Pi-Sunyer

Cast

ZEUS..Charlie Van Dyke
HERA..Tinsley Perica
ARES..Taylor Keller
APHRODITE..Saara Wallace
EROS..Brooke Soderbery
ATHENA..Anabelle Yujuico
THE SPHINX..Anna Pulendran
DIONYSUS..Josie Pleasants
HERMES..Josiah Flores
APOLLO..Chachi Boesen
HEPHAESTUS..Lucy Newton
POSEIDON..Owen Apfel
HESTIA..Brooke Soderbery
ARTEMIS..Tinsley Perica
HERCULES..John Plaschke
ARACHNE..Lucy Newton
DEMETER..Olivia Suarez
PERSEPHONE..Kiana Everett
HADES..Chachi Boesen
PANDORA..Paola Reinos

AUTHOR'S NOTE

I wrote this in the spring of 2020, when the whole world was under semi-quarantine due to the outbreak of COVID-19. Schools and theatres everywhere were canceling productions or looking for ways to perform plays online and there was a need for new plays that could be rehearsed and performed via video conference. My own kids' love of Greek mythology drove me to explore the idea of these all-powerful gods dealing with the same problem we mere mortals were facing. Finding new ways to portray these millennia-old characters was great fun and I have greatly enjoyed seeing young actors bring them to life in online productions. While this play was intended for that kind of performance, I think—from my vantage point watching hopefully for this crisis to end—***Greek Gods Under Quarantine*** could work just as well performed live in front of an audience as soon as it is safe to do so again.

I must give special thanks to my director, Rachel Prouty, who noticed that I had cut out the character of Dionysus, since middle schools usually don't want too many references to wine in plays performed by tweens. Rachel reminded me that Dionysus was also the god of theatre and I was thrilled to be able to bring him back in to the story in that mode.

Dean O'Carroll
January, 2021

(The play consists of video-chat conversations and is intended to be performed via Zoom or other video-conference technology.)

(ZEUS onscreen. Angry and imperious.)

(He has an almost empty pump of hand sanitizer. He is trying to get one last squirt out of it. It's not going well. After a few attempts, amid ad-libs, he gets very frustrated.)

ZEUS: So! That's the way it is, eh. Foolish hand sanitizer! Now you will face the wrath of Zeus!

(He raises a hand, about to strike the pump with lightning. He is interrupted by an alert sound.)

You have escaped with your life for now.

(Zeus clicks something. HERA appears in a new window. She is aloof and patrician.)

Hera! My queen, my wife!

HERA: Hello, dear. I'm just calling to check in with you. See how you're handling the quarantine. I got tired of playing Words with Friends with Thalia.

ZEUS: Thalia, the muse of comedy?

HERA: Yes. She always wants to banter in the chat. It's exhausting. So, beloved husband, master of the skies, hurler of lightning, how is social distancing treating you?

ZEUS: Not with the respect that should be afforded the King of Olympus, I will tell you that.

HERA: It's difficult on all of us, dear. I am the goddess of marriage after all, and Zoom weddings are just so gauche. "You may now text the bride a cute bitmoji"—"if anyone objects to this union, speak now or forever remain on mute." It's all just so déclassé, you know.

ZEUS: Is this even necessary? Are you certain this virus even affects gods and goddesses?

HERA: You can never be too careful, dear. The virus does seem to have a stronger effect on older people, and you and I are over 4000 years old.

ZEUS: I blame the mortals! You would think that a crisis like this would make mortals pay us a little more respect. Virus got you down? How about a little sacrifice for old Zeus? What have you got to lose? Remember the good old days, dear? Those little bugs used to worship us night and day. Now? Nothing!

HERA: The mortals moved on from us, dear. It's the way things go. We're still all over their art and language and…novels for middle readers.

ZEUS: The Norse thunder god gets to star in blockbuster movies? What do I get?

HERA: There is a planet named after you, dear.

ZEUS: After my Roman name! "Jupiter" was just a phase I was going through.

HERA: Like the man bun from a few years ago?

ZEUS: Exactly! Mortals! Disrespectful, disease-ridden, hubristic—

(An alert sound.)

HERA: Dear, as much as I would love to hear this rant for the ten thousandth time, one of our sons is calling me.

ZEUS: Which one, the blacksmith or GI Joe?

HERA: It's Ares, dear. I'll talk to you later.

ZEUS: Of course. *(To the hand sanitizer:)* Don't think I've forgotten about you!

(Zeus's window closes. ARES appears in a new window. He uses a front of regulated military authority to hide insecurity.)

ARES: Salutations, mother! Reporting for duty!

HERA: Hello, son. How is quarantine treating you?

ARES: Permission to speak freely?

HERA: ... Certainly.

ARES: It is a less than favorable situation for a war god. I do not enjoy going into combat against an enemy I cannot punch, stab or shoot. What am I supposed to do? Sit around playing *Call of Duty*?

HERA: So, what are you doing?

ARES: I'm...sitting around playing *Call of Duty*.

HERA: And also guarding the Hall of Important Stuff.

ARES: Of course! Yes! I am definitely in complete control over the Hall of Important Stuff.

HERA: That name does lack a certain *je ne sais quoi*. We really should find a better one. So everything in there is secure and accounted for?

ARES: Yes, mother. Everything currently in the Hall is secure and accounted for. The Golden Fleece. The Belt of Hippolyta. That first-generation video iPod Zeus filled up with episodes of *Ugly Betty* [feel free to update the reference, if desired].

HERA: Spare me the tiresome rundown. But I am a little curious why you said, "everything currently in the Hall."

ARES: Um...

HERA: Ares, you are a big boy now, so you do not need your mother checking up on you. But you know that Hall is full of important and powerful artifacts and if one of them was missing, well...people would talk.

ARES: Ma'am, yes, ma'am, I am aware.

HERA: The mortals are dealing with a serious virus right now. The last thing they need is some maniac getting ahold of Medusa's head or the Minotaur's horns or something like that and causing more trouble and strife on Earth.

ARES: Understood. If and when any such item were to be discovered to be missing, it would be of vital importance to—

HERA: Look. I am not in the mood to penetrate three layers of double-talk to find out exactly how you have botched this. If something is missing you need to get it back—immediately. You understand?

ARES: Yes, Mom. Right away!

(Hera's window disappears. Ares drops what's left of his military façade and panics. He quickly clicks and types.)

(APHRODITE answers. She is flirty and selfish.)

APHRODITE: Why, General! If I had known you were going to call, I would have put on my face. I must look a mess.

ARES: You look flawlessly beautiful as always, Aphrodite.

APHPRODITE: I know.

ARES: I need advice.

APHRODITE: Ooh! Romantic advice from the Goddess of Love? Is there a new girl in the picture? Now, I know it's hard to be affectionate during social distancing, but I can offer several hundred suggestions of how to—

ARES: Negative. The problem is not amorous in nature.

APHRODITE: Oh, pooh.

ARES: I may have been derelict in my duty in guarding the Hall of Important Stuff.

APHRODITE: Did somebody steal my back-issues of *Cosmo*? Tell me nobody stole my back issues of *Cosmo*!

ARES: I don't know! There was a disturbance and…I think something is missing. I'm not sure what. There's so much stuff in there! I can't keep track!

APHRODITE: How did this happen? Weren't you supposed to be guarding it?

ARES: I was… I subcontracted the job.

APHRODITE: To whom?

ARES: To…somebody with a very impressive record of being difficult to get past.

APHRODITE: Who? Cerberus? Ladon the dragon?

ARES: The Sphinx.

APHRODITE: Her? The one with the riddles? Ugh. I sat next to her at a banquet once and it was like hanging out with a second grader who just got his first joke book.

ARES: Well, I think she saw the thief but…

APHRODITE: But she'll only tell you through riddles.

ARES: I can't figure those things out. You know how I am with problems I can't stab.

APHRODITE: Poor little Ares.

ARES: So what do I do? My mother suspects something!

APHRODITE: Well, you know who could help you with this?

ARES: Don't say it.

APHRODITE: Athena.

ARES: Athena. Athena. Athena. Always Dad's favorite. She gets the capital of Greece named after her. She gets the giant temple at the Acropolis.

APHRODITE: You do have a planet named after you.

ARES: Yeah, after my Roman name. Did you see that *John Carter of Mars* movie they made? Yuck.

APHRODITE: Well, you're not going to solve any riddles yourself, and I'm certainly not going to give myself wrinkles by furrowing my brow in thought.

ARES: Could...you call her?

APHRODITE: Oh, you know old gray-eyes and I don't get along. That armor she wears, season after season? Don't get me started.

ARES: Please? Please please please please please?

APHRODITE: Oh...all right. I won't call her myself, but I can get someone to do it.

ARES: Thank you!

APHRODITE: Don't mention it. I love a man in uniform. Bye.

(She clicks. Ares' window disappears. Aphrodite clicks again and EROS appears in a new window. A sulky adolescent. Wings on his shoulders, if possible.)

EROS: Hi, Mom.

APHRODITE: You sound a bit moody today, Eros.

EROS: Mom, for literally the millionth time, I prefer my Roman name.

APHRODITE: But honey, when people hear "Cupid" they think of a chubby baby in a diaper on a valentine. Eros is a much more mature name.

EROS: Why are you calling, Mom?

APHRODITE: Well, now I'm calling to find out why you're so grouchy today.

EROS: Because I'm stuck here, Mom! This stupid quarantine! Do you know how long it's been since I got to shoot mortals with my love arrows?

APHRODITE: I feel it too, honey. These poor mortals. There's only so much they can do over text. I have tried to spread my blessings to try to add romance to a few Zoom sessions, of course, but it's not the same.

EROS: Yeah. Even if I could make somebody fall in love with somebody, what are they going to do? Shout poetry at each other from six feet away? This virus really ruffles my wings.

APHRODITE: Well, I have a project for you. Someone stole something from the Hall of Important Stuff, but only the Sphinx knows who.

EROS: The Sphinx? Oh, Mom, I can't do riddles.

APHRODITE: Honey, love is the ultimate riddle.

EROS: Weak, Mom.

APHRODITE: I just want you to ask your Auntie Athena to try to talk to the Sphinx.

EROS: Why me? Just because you hate her?

APHRODITE: I don't hate anybody! I am the goddess of love! For example, with Athena...I just love the way she doesn't care what she looks like.

EROS: Yeah, I guess I can do that. Athena's kinda cool in a "while we've been talking I've already figured out thirteen ways to defeat you" kind of way.

APHRODITE: Thanks, sweetie. Oh, and you're wearing a mask when you go out and washing your hands and everything, right?

EROS: *(Sighs:)* Yes, Mom.

APHRODITE: That's my boy.

(Aphrodite clicks and her window vanishes. Eros clicks. ATHENA appears in a new window. Cool, bright, witty, a little arrogant.)

ATHENA: Hey, Feathers.

EROS: Hey, Athena. So, like, my mom needs your help or whatever.

ATHENA: The Love Dove needs little old me?

EROS: You know that, like, cat lady, the Sphinx? She saw somebody steal something from the Hall of Important Junk, but she'll only tell you what she saw if you solve a riddle.

ATHENA: So you came to the only one around here with any brains?

EROS: Uh...yeah, pretty much.

ATHENA: All right, I guess I can delay my third consecutive *Parks and Recreation* binge-watch. Thanks for the heads-up, Hawkeye.

EROS: Sure, yeah, whatever. Bye.

(Eros's window closes. Athena clicks. THE SPHINX, cat-like and secretive, appears in a window.)

SPHINX: Purr.

ATHENA: That's how you greet the goddess of wisdom?

SPHINX: That's how I greet everyone. I'm a cat-woman.

ATHENA: I understand you know who robbed the Hall?

SPHINX: Does anyone really "understand"?

ATHENA: Do you know?

SPHINX: Only who it was, not what was taken.

ATHENA: Just give me the riddle.

SPHINX: You really think you can solve my riddle?

ATHENA: Is this the old riddle that Oedipus solved?

SPHINX: This riddle beats that one with a two-by-four.

ATHENA: What's the riddle?

SPHINX: You may not catch me at home, but I can catch you, and perhaps you and I can share, in short.

ATHENA: Hmm...

SPHINX: You're going to love this one, goddess of many things.

ATHENA: You don't need to give me extra hints.

SPHINX: You think I'm giving you extra hints? That's your interpretation.

ATHENA: You mean my spin?

SPHINX: ...um...

ATHENA: I had it when you said this beats your last riddle with a two-by-four.

SPHINX: But that wasn't—

ATHENA: Of course it was. Your classic riddle was "What walks on four legs in the morning, two in the afternoon, and three at night." The answer is "humans"—they crawl on all fours as babies, walk on two legs as adults, and walk with two legs and a cane as seniors. Anyway, you said this riddle beats that one with a two-by-four. Two times four equals eight. So humans have four, two or three legs, but this has eight? And it might catch me in its home? And you and I share "in short," so "we have" becomes "we've," which sounds like "weave" like a weaver? And it puts a "spin" on things? It's a spider.

SPHINX: You! Oh!

ATHENA: And, since you took special relish in it being me trying to solve this particular riddle, I know which spider.

SPHINX: You may have solved this one, but my next riddle will be—

ATHENA: Sure. You do that. Bye.

(Athena clicks. Sphinx's window disappears. Athena sighs.)

First things first.

(Athena clicks. DIONYSUS appears in a window. He is ostentatiously theatrical.)

DIONYSUS: Greetings! Hail and well met!

ATHENA: Oh...Dionysus. You're in god-of-theatre mode today.

DIONYSUS: Indeed. I awoke this morning feeling most theatrical.

ATHENA: That's great. I know all about being the god of multiple domains, but I was kind of hoping you'd be in god-of-wine mode today. I was feeling like talking about my problems with a friendly bartender.

DIONYSUS: Sorry. Since I am in my role as a vessel for the drama I cannot imbibe today, lest I do harm to my instrument. But you are in luck.

ATHENA: Why do I doubt that?

DIONYSUS: I may not be the bartender you seek, but, as a master thespian I can assay the role of a friendly barkeep! It shall be a triumph!

ATHENA: Okay. I guess you won't be the first actor who has to work as a bartender on the side.

DIONYSUS: Let me get into character.

(Dionysus does some stretches and vocal exercises.)

ATHENA: Take your time. It's not like the fate of the universe might be at stake.

DIONYSUS: Big black bugs bleed blue-black blood. There! Ready!

ATHENA: Okay, so—

DIONYSUS: Wait! Costume!

(Dionysus puts on an apron and begins wiping a glass with a dishrag.)

Hello! Welcome to my tavern! What libation may I pour for you, customer? I say! Your brow looks troubled. Please, pour forth your worries as I pour forth your drink.

ATHENA: You remember the story of Arachne?

DIONYSUS: Was that one by Aeschylus? Sophocles? Euripides?

ATHENA: It's not a play. It's something that...was my fault. Arachne is the woman who became a spider.

DIONYSUS: Ah yes! That one I know! With great power comes great responsibility!

ATHENA: That's Spider-Man. Arachne was a weaver, probably the greatest mortal weaver of all time.

DIONYSUS: But, as I recall, among your other specialties, you are the goddess of weaving.

ATHENA: Crafts in general. But this human Arachne thought she was better than me. And...well, I couldn't let that slide. Long story short, I turned her into a spider.

DIONYSUS: Ah, the mistakes we made when we were young! I recall a young actor who thought his turn as Agamemnon rivaled my own! I turned him into a raisin and he was baked into a cookie by an unsuspecting grandmother.

ATHENA: Arachne is still around, and she hates the gods for what I did to her. She stole something from the Hall of Important Stuff, and she might be trying to do something dangerous.

DIONYSUS: A dilemma worthy of the finest dramatists.

ATHENA: I feel like this is all my fault.

DIONYSUS: Be that as it may, you are not alone in solving this crisis. You are but one character in this drama! You are part of a family of gods and goddesses, and we will stand with you until the final curtain!

ATHENA: Well, that's true. So who can help me catch her? With all due respect, that seems a bit out of your wheelhouse.

DIONYSUS: My dear, there is no character that is beyond me. I could play a spider catcher with such pathos it would make the heavens weep! But I will concede there may be others here on Mount Olympus better suited to the practical task of apprehending a bandit. You know the old saying, "it takes a thief to catch a thief"? And, as I recall, a brother of ours is the god of thieves.

ATHENA: So I call Hermes?

DIONYSUS: No. I shall call him! Your statement that pursuing Arachne is "not in my wheelhouse" has spurred me to prove myself. Now I shall don the deerstalker cap and assume the role of sleuth. Perhaps this shall be my greatest tour de force.

ATHENA: Dionysus, did I hurt your feelings?

DIONYSUS: I fear you have cut me to the quick. That you would suggest there is a role I could not play? My heart is wounded perhaps beyond repair.

(He sinks, looking very sad.)

ATHENA: Hey, I'm sorry.

DIONYSUS: Boo hoo hoo. Boo hoo hoo.

ATHENA: I didn't mean to... I mean, I didn't know this would—

(Dionysus snaps out of it. He was only faking.)

DIONYSUS: Acting!

ATHENA: Genius.

DIONYSUS: Thank you! And now! You may take your exit!

(Dionysus clicks. Athena's window closes.)

"To sit in solemn silence on a dull dark dock." Oh, who am I kidding? I'm always prepared.

(HERMES appears on a new window. He is a fast talker.)

HERMES: Dionysus! How's it going? How's quarantine treating you? You good? You look good. Have you lost weight? Me, I've put on a few. Too much baking. Have you tried a sourdough starter? Boy, are those things hard.

DIONYSUS: Slow down, slow down! By the ghost of Thespis, you speak your words, dare I say, too trippingly on the tongue!

HERMES: Sorry. Sorry. It's the quarantine. It's driving me nuts! I'm used to zipping around the world delivering messages! Travelling! Getting out of the house! Now I'm bouncing off the walls. Nobody's sending messages! It's all Skype and Zoom and Shloom and whatever.

DIONYSUS: Yes, well...hmm... I think I need a costume piece for this.

(Dionysus puts on a fedora. He now tries to assume the role of a TV cop.)

All right, ya mook. You know why we brought you down here.

HERMES: What's going on right now?

DIONSYSUS: One of your dirtbag criminal buddies made off with something from the Hall of Important Stuff, and I'm going to squeeze your shoes until you tell me how to catch her.

HERMES: What are you talking about?

DIONYSUS: Are you or are you not the god of thieves?

HERMES: Whoah whoah whoah whoah! I'm the god of a lot of things, bro! I'm the god of messengers. I'm the god of trade. I'm the god of travelers. I'm the god of sports. I'm the god of border crossings. I'm the god of shepherds. I'm the god of orators. I'm the god of wit. I'm the god of literature. I'm the god of invention.

DIONYSUS: And thieves.

HERMES: Yeah, I think they're in there somewhere.

DIONYSUS: Are you gonna spill, wing-head, or do I gotta turn up the heat? What did Arachne take?

HERMES: Arachne the spider? She stole something? That's not like her. She's a trapper, not a thief. She's working for somebody.

(Dionysus drops the cop character.)

DIONYSUS: Oh! The plot thickens.

HERMES: So who hires a spider? What was the hierarchy in that old song? The old woman swallows a fly, then a spider…she swallows a bird to catch the spider…that wriggles and jiggles and wiggles inside her. But how absurd to swallow a bird.

DIONYSUS: Dear boy, you're singing a number they should have cut in New Haven. If we catch her, then we can ask who hired her.

HERMES: Okay, well, to catch her we need a hunter. We need…Artemis! Oh! Can I call her?

DIONYSUS: Well, I…I suppose.

HERMES: A message! I can send a message! Yes! All right! Will do! And if you never need any help stealing anything, just ask.

DIONYSUS: My boy, the only thing I ever steal is the show! And with that, I ring down the curtain!

(He bows and clicks. His window closes.)

HERMES: Um…bye.

(Hermes clicks. APOLLO appears in a new window. He is a surfer-poet with a SoCal accent.)

APOLLO: Hermes! My excellent compatriot! It is most righteous to see you.

HERMES: Hi, Apollo. I was expecting your twin sister.

APOLLO: Artemis and I are quarantining together. God of the sun and Goddess of the moon. A most harmonious pairing, is it not? Yet, alas, she has of late taken to making long sojourns out of the house alone.

HERMES: Yeah, I can't imagine why anyone would want to leave the house when you're in it.

APOLLO: But fear not, my winged-helmeted brother. Artemis is taking great care to abide by the laws laid down by our father, the almighty Zeus, and fully endorsed by me, the god of healing. She is always masked, and since her weapon of choice is the arrow, she maintains a safe distance from all living things until she kills them. She always washes her hands thoroughly upon returning to our home and then self-quarantines in her room for several hours, longer if I am practicing on my lyre. But—

HERMES: It is very important that I locate Artemis! Arachne the spider has stolen something important, and we need Artemis to track her and capture her.

APOLLO: Oh! A most perplexing dilemma! For though my sister has caught many a deer or bear or grouse, has she ever wrangled a creature of the eight-legged variety? I know not.

HERMES: Please stay focused. Where can I find Artemis?

APOLLO: She will need swift transport for this mission. And since she lacks your triumphant winged sandals, I shall loan her the use of my thoroughly gnarly sun chariot.

HERMES: Okay great, but where—

APOLLO: —But alas, my chariot is in the shop, for I have taken this chance to have Hephaestus trick it out with all the latest awesome accoutrements. I must call our mechanically-inclined half-brother and ask if his endeavors have reached their most excellent climax.

HERMES: Please just tell me where I can reach Artemis!

APOLLO: Oh—she's in the woods, but she has her mobile.

HERMES: Thanks, bye.

(Hermes' window disappears. Apollo clicks and HEPHAESTUS appears. He has a Boston accent.)

HEPHAESTUS: Hello, caller. Talk to me.

APOLLO: Hephaestus, most excellent blacksmith! How fare you during this most heinous time of plague?

HEPHAESTUS: I tell you, sunshine, it's not that hard for me. I stay here in my workshop, dawn till dark, bangin' out sparks, makin' my mark. It's a walk in the park. You know, making parts for carts. Eros needs heart darts. Orders are off the charts.

But my life is my art— Oh, hey, here's something that occurred to me the other day—aren't you the god of plague?

APOLLO: Indeed. I am both the god of plague and the god of healing. It is a most perplexing duality.

HEPHAESTUS: So does that mean you're the one to blame for all of this?

APOLLO: Most assuredly not, my iron-bending bro. I lost my interest in plagues many centuries ago. That one with the rats back in the 1300s was so thoroughly nasty that I no longer find it amusing to spread disease and death.

HEPHAESTUS: So those mortals gotta take responsibility for this one themselves, huh? Well, that's a puzzler.

APOLLO: But one that can be managed. Wear masks, maintain distance, wash hands.

HEPHAESTUS: Yeah, I been washing mine wicked hard. Turns out I have skin under all this grease and oil. Coulda knocked me over with a feather. Anyway, you callin' about your car? I added the smart park, the dash cam and the in-chariot wi-fi. You also have Siri, Alexa and Cortana. But I still need to add the mag wheels, the rim-saver tires and four more cup holders.

APOLLO: Righteous! Well, I am in need of my chariot posthaste, for my twin sister will need supersonic transportation on her next hunt, to capture the dastardly Arachne, who has absconded with an unknown item from the Hall of Awesomely Important Stuff.

HEPHAESTUS: Oh, that does sound wicked important. Okay, I can get your car road-ready in under an hour, but first I gotta call Poseidon. He's been all over me to fix that luxury barge of his and I gotta put him off.

APOLLO: Muchas gracias, hermano. I will inform my twin sister that her chariot awaits.

HEPHAESTUS: Yeah, just give her one piece of advice for when she gets behind the wheel.

APOLLO: What's that?

HEPHAESTUS: Don't drive like my brother.

(Apollo looks perplexed as his window closes. Hephaestus clicks. POSEIDON appears in a new window. He is a wealthy sailing enthusiast.)

POSEIDON: Ahoy there. Nephew, you're looking smashing. That whole grimy workman look…it's just so…you.

HEPHAESTUS: Yeah, thanks, Cap'n. How are things under the water?

POSEIDON: Oh, things are going swimmingly. Little joke there I heard from one of the nereids. We're all well. The ocean is pretty safe from this dreadful little virus you're dealing with. Plus, fewer humans mucking about in the waters makes it much cleaner. But I do miss seeing their little ships around and frightening them with shark attacks and tsunamis. You know. The little things. And how is Olympus handling this?

HEPHAESTUS: Oh, things are pretty bizarre in our fair city. A couple of us are gettin' cabin fever. Ganymede the cup bearer's shattered like fourteen chalices out of pure frustration. But everybody's being responsible. We even got Narcissus to wear a mask, and that was harder than a harpy's heart.

POSEIDON: So, what's the good word old chum? Is my lovely tub all shipshape and seaworthy?

HEPHAESTUS: Well, that's why I'm calling. I got a rush job, so yours is gonna be delayed.

POSEIDON: Oh, bother! I had my heart set on taking her out on the Aegean tomorrow. Why couldn't you have finished this earlier?

HEPHAESTUS: Sorry, Skipper, but this barge isn't some backwater schooner I could fix in a fortnight.

POSEIDON: Oh, very well. I really feel like I should talk to your manager about this.

HEPHAESTUS: My only manager is my father, Zeus. You really want to pester your brother about this?

POSEIDON: All right, all right. Do what you need to do for the Bobsey Twins. I have other projects.

HEPHAESTUS: Let me guess—you gotta plan the Key Largo Escargot Car Show and Clam Chowder Baking Powder Power Hour?

POSEIDON: That's not till next month.

HEPHAESTUS: Don't worry, I'll get your barge on the water before you can say "submarine fugitive." And, even though it makes the goddess Nike want to say "just *don't* do it," this is HPR—Hephaestus's Personal Repairs.

(Hephaestus clicks and his window closes.)

POSEIDON: Well, I didn't understand that last bit at all. Never mind.

(Poseidon pouts. His window goes blank briefly and a window reading "One Hour Later" appears. Back up on Poseidon still stewing. An alert sound. He clicks to answer it. HESTIA appears, a home decoration DIY expert.)

Hestia. Ahoy and pip pip and all that.

HESTIA: I'm calling because I was hoping to get some coral and abalone shells for a decoupage project, but you seem to be out of sorts.

POSEIDON: Well, dear goddess of the hearth, I'm having a simply dreadful day. I can't get my boat fixed because Artemis needs the sun chariot to go spider hunting or some such and it's really just put a barnacle on my hull!

HESTIA: I'm sorry, what was that?

POSEIDON: Oh, I don't know the details. But apparently what's-her-name, Arachy-Wacky, stole something from that Hall where Zeus keeps all his favorite trinkets and Artemis is off hunting her.

HESTIA: So our niece is battling an immortal spider, possibly to save humanity from doom, and you're upset about your boat?

POSEIDON: You have to understand: I really love this boat.

HESTIA: I'm going to have to call you back. I want to make sure Artemis is all right. I care deeply for her. She catches all my pheasants for me.

POSEIDON: Well, all right, if you must. I guess it's another night of binge-watching on Netfish for me. You know, as the sea god, I invented streaming.

HESTIA: And you should feel very proud about that.

(Poseidon vanishes. Hestia clicks and ARTEMIS appears. She seems to be outdoors and is wiping cobwebs off herself. She is sporty and tough.)

ARTEMIS: Hey, Aunt Hestie! How's it going?

HESTIA: I'm well, thank you. But I was a bit concerned when I heard you were trying to capture Arachne.

ARTEMIS: Oh, I appreciate that. But that's done and done. All that's left is getting these webs off me. I tracked her, caught her, bagged her and brought her back to a holding cell. It was a little harder because I had the mask on, and gloves, and had to stop to wash my hands immediately afterwards. Took me fifteen whole minutes. Longest hunt I've had in years. Quarantine must be making me soft.

HESTIA: Dear, that's really very impressive. I think someone has earned herself a basket of decorative gourds.

ARTEMIS: Well, thanks. Actually, part of me wishes it took longer. Once I get home I know a certain god of music, who happens to be my twin brother, is going to want to perform his one-man *Hamilton* for me...again.

HESTIA: Did you find out what Arachne stole? I had some very precious embroidered potholders in there, and I hate to think she got webs on them.

ARTEMIS: No, that's the problem. She won't talk. I can't interrogate anyone to save my life. Usually once I'm done hunting something, they're not exactly capable of talking, you know what I mean? By the way, I caught you three quail, two wild turkeys and an elk. I'll leave them on your back porch.

HESTIA: Thank you, I'll make a stew. Well, we need to find out what she took and who told her to take it. You may need to—what do humans say?—play "bad cop"?

ARTEMIS: Sorry, Hes. I can't do it. I can't be bad cop to a spider. Too much respect for them as a species. Too vital to the natural balance. But...I suppose we could call in the ultimate bad cop. The guy who could crush a whole army of spiders by looking at them funny. He could put the scare into her.

HESTIA: Oh. Well, I'll leave that up to you. I should check if my hive-fresh beeswax candles have cooled. Goodbye and good luck.

ARTEMIS: Catch you.

(Hestia's window closes. Artemis clicks. A blank window appears. Out of sight on this new window, HERCULES is doing push-ups. Perhaps his head pops in and out of view as he counts.)

HERCULES: Eleven thousand nine hundred and ninety-eight. Eleven thousand nine hundred and ninety-nine.

ARTEMIS: Hello? Hercules? Are you there?

HERCULES: Twelve thousand!

(He sits up, fully visible now. He has a barbell and starts doing curls. He is macho and, while not dumb, far from cerebral.)

HERCULES: Hey. Sorry. Had to get my reps in. You're looking good. You doing keto?

ARTEMIS: Just lots of running and archery.

HERCULES: So, like, CrossFit?

ARTEMIS: Sort of. Look, Herc, I need your help.

HERCULES: Yeah. I can help. I'm a huge hero.

ARTEMIS: What I need you to do is... Could you stop curling for a minute?

HERCULES: No can do. Can't let up the pace just 'cause I'm in quarantine. Hephaestus made these for me special. They're 12 tons each.

ARTEMIS: Look, Muscles, I captured Arachne and I need you to interrogate her to find out what she stole from the Hall of Important Stuff.

HERCULES: So! The mighty huntress needs to bring in a big strong man to crush a spider for her? You're like a sitcom housewife leaping on a chair when she sees a creepy crawly.

ARTEMIS: Hey, remind me again, when you were mortal, you killed all those monsters, but what was it that finally killed you?

HERCULES: Oh, my, uh...mortal wife smeared the wrong potion on my cloak and it poisoned me.

ARTEMIS: Yeah, a woman accidentally killed you in a laundry mishap. So maybe knock it off about sitcom housewives and keep your mouth shut before I shoot you so full of arrows you look like an electrified porcupine.

HERCULES: Uh...okay. So you just need me to question Arachne?

ARTEMIS: Much better. I'll patch you through.

(Artemis clicks. Her window disappears and ARACHNE, devious and spiteful, appears in a new window. She could be a spider puppet or an actress in some spidery costume.)

HERCULES: Hey, Legs.

ARACHNE: You? You are the one they sent into my parlor? Did they really think your musclebound brain could match wits with my web of wisdom?

HERCULES: No, probably not. I think they just thought you'd be afraid I'd squash you.

ARACHNE: You can't get near me. You're under quarantine.

HERCULES: Oh, that's true. Funny, because there are some spiders here in my place and they're just so easy to squish.

(He starts squishing spiders, out of camera range.)

There's one. There's another one.

ARACHNE: Hey! Stop that! You need spiders! They eat bugs! You want your house overrun by bugs? You need spiders!

HERCULES: Yeah, but I—splat!—also need you to tell me what you—splat!—took from the Hall and you're—splat!—not telling what that is, so…splat!

ARACHNE: Fine! Fine! I'll tell you! I'll tell you! It's Pandora's Box! Pandora's Box!

HERCULES: There, now was that so hard? So where's this box you stole?

ARACHNE: I already handed it off to the person who hired me to steal it. But before you start killing any more innocent spiders, I don't know who it was! It was an anonymous transaction!

HERCULES: Are you—splat!—sure you don't know?

ARACHNE: I swear! I swear!

HERCULES: All right. Well, I guess you've been a little helpful.

ARACHNE: You're a murderer!

HERCULES: Actually, those things I was squishing were raisins. Glad you fell for it, though. See you later, Legs.

(Arachne sputters furiously as her window closes.)

Now what on Olympus is Pandoro's Box? Hey, Alexa, what's Pandoro?

(A computer voice is heard in Hercules's window.)

COMPUTER VOICE: Pandoro is a traditional Italian sweetbread, most commonly eaten around Christmas.

HERCULES: Bread, huh. Okay. I know who to ask about that.

(He clicks. DEMETER appears in a new window. An older flower child.)

DEMETER: Hercules! It's so groovy to hear from you.

HERCULES: Hey Demeter. So you're the goddess of grain, right?

DEMETER: Right on. I'm the goddess of grain and the harvest and, just, all the beautiful bounty that Mother Earth bestows on us. Oh—this virus is just so uncool—I wish you could be here in person so we could really vibe together. I have a delicious kombucha I'd love to share.

HERCULES: Yeah. Well, I don't know anything about breads and grains because I stay away from carbs. But somebody hired Arachne to steal some kind of bread box from the Hall of Important Stuff. Is that a big deal?

DEMETER: A bread box?

HERCULES: Yeah, Pandoro's Box, I think.

DEMETER: Pandor-O?

HERCULES: Yeah. Italian people eat it at Christmas?

DEMETER: Do you mean Pandora's Box?

HERCULES: Yeah. Maybe that was it. What is that?

DEMETER: This is so far out! You don't know the story of Pandora's Box?

HERCULES: I kinda tune out when someone tells me a story that doesn't have a lot of punching and killing in it.

DEMETER: It's a bummer story, man. Pandora was a girl sent to Earth with a box that the gods told her never to open. But one day she did and suddenly all the problems of the world came flying out: hatred, war, famine, jealousy, disease...bad vibes...runny tie-dye. It was the worst.

HERCULES: So...that sounds bad.

DEMETER: Pandora's Box could harsh even the most mellow of mellows. But I thought it was…

HERCULES: Look, is there anything I can do? Is there something I should be punching?

DEMETER: Violence doesn't solve problems.

HERCULES: Every problem in my life has been caused and solved by violence.

DEMETER: After this is over, I'm going to send you some herbal teas and therapy candles, but now I need to call somebody.

HERCULES: Okay. Let me know when the punching starts.

(Hercules' window closes. Demeter clicks. PERSEPHONE appears. She is similar to her mother, with perhaps a bit of a Valley Girl vibe.)

PERSEPHONE: Hey Mom! How are you today?

DEMETER: Persephone, it is so beautiful to see you.

PERSEPHONE: It's, like, so beautiful to see you, too, Mom! But this virus is such a buzzkill!

DEMETER: I know!

PERSEPHONE: I know!

DEMETER: I mean, like, I never get to see you face-to-face now, and usually I only get to see you half of the year anyway because of this fascist rule Zeus made that you have to spend the other half with your husband.

PERSEPHONE: It's bogus. I know.

DEMETER: I know.

PERSEPHONE: Y'know?

DEMETER: I know.

PERSEPHONE: But Hades and I…we have like our own thing and we make it work, you know?

DEMETER: I know.

PERSEPHONE: Y'know?

DEMETER: I know. Listen, Dewdrop, I need you to talk to your husband. It's about a dead girl.

PERSEPHONE: Oh, yeah, like, he knows a lot of dead girls.

DEMETER: It's about Pandora.

PERSEPHONE: Oh, yeah. She died like a million years ago. I think Hades had her in Tartarus for punishment because she, like, y'know, opened that box and unleashed all this terrible junk into the world? But that seemed, like, totally unfair because we gods kind of tricked her into doing it? So I got him to move her to the Elysian Fields.

DEMETER: Oh, Starchild, that's so nice of you.

PERSEPHONE: Yeah, I totally got him to move a bunch of people out of Tartarus. Now it's just really, really bad people like murderers and dictators and that guy who invented wearing skirts over jeans?

DEMETER: Okay, but you need to get him to rap with Pandora. Somebody has her box and I'm worried they'll use it to unleash even more bad vibes on the Earth and those mortals can't take any more bad vibes right now. You know?

PERSEPHONE: I know! Y'now?

DEMETER: I know!

PERSEPHONE: But I thought that box was, like, empty now.

DEMETER: I know, but what if it wasn't?

PERSEPHONE: Mom. You just, like, totally blew my mind.

DEMETER: I know.

PERSEPHONE: I know!

DEMETER: I know.

PERSEPHONE: Sure, Mom, I'll call Hades.

DEMETER: Thanks, Rainwhisper. Are we still on for the Zoom drum circle with the Anemoi tomorrow? Y'know, assuming the world hasn't ended?

PERSEPHONE: Wouldn't miss it, Mom! Bye-ee!

DEMETER: Bye-ee!

(Demeter's window closes. Persephone clicks. HADES appears. He is gloomy and goth-like.)

HADES: Hi.

PERSEPHONE: Hi Hades! How's my hubby today?

HADES: I sit in darkness, contemplating the futility of existence.

PERSEPHONE: But that's like your favorite thing to do.

HADES: Yeah. It's okay. You don't usually call me during this part of the year.

PERSEPHONE: That's not true! I totally send you postcards from all the awesome outdoor stuff I do during the six months I'm not trapped in the Underworld with you!

HADES: Trapped? Aren't we all?

PERSEPHONE: I didn't mean that. So…how is the Underworld with all of this going on? I mean, like, so many people are, like—

HADES: No! No! I don't want people to die! Not of terrible diseases anyway. We have enough spirits down here. Plus…this place is getting so phony.

PERSEPHONE: The afterlife is getting phony?

HADES: The River Styx totally went mainstream. You wouldn't understand.

PERSEPHONE: So, honey, here's the issue. You need to talk to Pandora. Somebody stole her box and, like, might unleash some heinous stuff on Earth.

HADES: Pandora's Box wasn't so bad. It had, y'know, despair and ennui and stuff in it. Those are okay.

PERSEPHONE: Honey, please?

HADES: ...anything for you, Persephone.

PERSEPHONE: You are such a softy under all that black.

HADES: Okay, just don't tell anybody.

PERSEPHONE: Okay, I'm gonna go make three million daisy chains now. I'll send you some. Bye-ee!

HADES: Yeah.

(Persephone's window closes. Hades gestures. Perhaps there is some magical audio effect. PANDORA, kind and strong, appears in a new window.)

PANDORA: Where I am? What's going on?

HADES: Yeah, so, Pandora, I had to yank you out of the Elysian Fields for a while. I guess I'm "sorry" to interrupt your, *(Small dismissive grunt:)* unending happiness or whatever.

PANDORA: Oh. Yeah. I was just enjoying the sensation of realizing you're in love with someone for the first time, over and over again, for the past fifty-seven years.

HADES: Yeah. I guess a lot of people like that one.

PANDORA: But, what do you need, almighty master of the Underworld?

HADES: You know that box that you used to have that, you know, ruined the world or whatever? Somebody took it.

PANDORA: What? Who did that?

HADES: I mean, isn't that thing empty now? Or is there, like, extra bad stuff in there? Like…double famine or something? Or, I had this idea for a thing where it's kinda like war but also itchy.

PANDORA: The box is empty, except for one thing. Lord Hades, I think I know who did this.

HADES: So what do you need? Want me to send Cerberus to chew his head off?

PANDORA: No. I just want to talk with him.

HADES: Yeah, sure. Just think the name and he'll appear on a window before you. Do what you need to do and then you can go back to being dead…y'know, unless this all ends in the universe getting destroyed. Oh…hey…for just a split second that thought of the universe getting destroyed made me happy. Didn't know I could still feel that. Okay, good luck. Or maybe not. Whatever.

(Hades' window disappears.)

PANDORA: Thief? This is Pandora. Show yourself.

(A new window appears. It is blank.)

Show yourself. I'm not afraid of you. I've been dead for thousands of years.

(In the blank window, Zeus enters or appears.)

ZEUS: So. You figured out I took your box.

PANDORA: You're the only one who would, Zeus.

(Zeus shows that he has the box.)

ZEUS: You remember why we sent you to Earth with this in the first place?

PANDORA: You thought humans were getting too proud and too accomplished.

ZEUS: Too much like the gods.

PANDORA: That's why you cursed me with curiosity so I would unleash all the gods' failings, too—your wrath, Hera's jealousy, Ares' love of war, Aphrodite's vanity. You made mortals just as bad as you all are.

ZEUS: That's not the way I would put it.

PANDORA: But all those horrors flew out of the box thousands of years ago. If you wanted to send more problems to Earth, you won't find them in there.

ZEUS: No. There's only one thing left in the box, and you know what it is.

PANDORA: The one thing box you didn't account for: hope. Underneath all the horrors, there was hope. And it's that hope that has let humans get through all the other terrible things. They always have some hope that things could get better.

ZEUS: A rare mistake on my part. That stupid hope. That stupid little thing that keeps them from abject despair. Without that hope, they'd be begging the gods for mercy all day long. I miss the begging so much. But they think they don't need us anymore because, in spite of it all, they still have their precious hope.

PANDORA: And they always will.

ZEUS: Ugh. I thought the hope had flown out of the box, too, but there's still some in there.

PANDORA: It's an inexhaustible resource.

ZEUS: Well, not anymore.

PANDORA: So I was right? That's why you stole the box. To kill hope?

ZEUS: Exactly. I always said humans were hopeless. Now let's make that true. This virus has taken so much from them, but they still have that stupid hope keeping them going. That ends now. I've been waiting for an audience, and you're the perfect one. I'm going to crush this last iota of hope and watch how the humans come crawling back to us.

PANDORA: That's not going to happen, Lord Zeus.

ZEUS: Let's find out.

(Zeus seems to be throttling or crushing something inside the box.)

This is a bit tougher than I thought.

(Zeus gestures with a finger. There is a thunderclap sound and, if possible, a lightning effect from the box.)

Will you just die already?

PANDORA: No. It won't.

ZEUS: Why not?

PANDORA: Even you can't kill hope. It's too much a part of what humans are.

ZEUS: Then maybe we do this the old-fashioned way! Maybe it's time to dust off the old thunderbolt and start scorching some ungrateful human hides!

(Zeus holds up a threatening looking bolt of lightning.)

PANDORA: I think some people might have something to say about that.

(Hera, Ares, Aphrodite, Eros, Athena, Dionysus, Hermes, Apollo, Hephaestus, Poseidon, Hestia, Artemis, Hercules, Demeter, Persephone and Hades appear in individual windows. They are all unhappy. Ad-lib greetings of "Zeus" from [Hera, Aphrodite and Eros] "Father/Dad" [from Ares, Athena, Dionysus, Hermes, Hephaestus, Artemis, Hercules and Persephone] or "Brother" [from Poseidon, Hestia, Demeter and Hades] all overlap as the window populates. You can have Sphinx and Arachne appear, too, though they shouldn't speak, instead pouting sullenly. Not every character needs to appear, if you would prefer. If you have double-cast any of these roles, the performer can choose whichever character they prefer. Similarly, if it is not technically feasible for your production to include the full cast, you could pick just a handful of characters to appear, though Hera should definitely be present, even if the performer is double-cast. You can adjust the following dialogue as necessary:)

ZEUS: Hello…everyone.

HERA: Dear, were you just about to destroy humanity?

ZEUS: And what if I was?

(Ad-lib objections from everyone. Some of the following lines could be used. They may overlap. Do not use all of the lines unless you choose to have them all spoken simultaneously to create a cacophony.)

HERA: We have been over this, dear. Humans may not worship us anymore, but they're the ones keeping our memories alive. If you kill them all, who's going to maintain all our old statues and temples? The cockroaches?

ARES: Dad! Don't destroy them! They're so good at destroying themselves!

APHRODITE: Zeus, surely a wise, handsome King of the Gods like you doesn't need to bully some poor mortals.

EROS: Not cool, Zeus!

ATHENA: Father, can we discuss whether this is really the wisest move from a tactical standpoint? Spoiler alert: no.

DIONYSUS: I pray, Father. Do not ring down the curtain on these wretched mortals for they…they are our audience.

HERMES: *(Super fast:)* DaddaddaddaddadDAD! Think about this, this is madness, this is crazy! You don't want to kill mortals! We love mortals!

(More of the same, ad-lib.)

APOLLO: Father! This is most heinously uncool! May I respectfully recommend that you chill to a fine mellow, with mucho rapidity?

HEPHAESTUS: Hey, Father, you're being wicked hard on these mortals.

POSEIDON: Old sport, this dreadfully uncouth. Shape up or ship out.

HESTIA: This is quite ungracious, Brother.

ARTEMIS: C'mon, Dad. You'd hate yourself in the morning.

HERCULES: Dad, everybody knows you've got lightning. But killing mortals? Weird flex, bro.

DEMETER: Zeus, I really think you need to just decompress, maybe drink some matcha and just get your head in the right place before you take action.

PERSEPHONE: This is, like, so randomly aggressive, Daddy. You know?

DEMETER: I know!

PERSEPHONE: I know!

HADES: Knock it off, brother. I do not want to do the paperwork for seven billion new souls.

(After everyone is finished...)

ZEUS: Fine! Fine! I won't destroy humanity. And I'll let them have their hope, *if*...you all pretend I never tried this and you promise that I will face no consequences for my actions.

(Groans from all the others.)

ATHENA: Well, that is how pretty much every story about you ends.

DIONYSUS: A familiar-perhaps-hackneyed denouement, but not without its own traditionalist charm.

HEPHAESTUS: If it ain't broke, don't fix it, eh, Father?

HERA: Quiet, quiet down all. I suppose we can look the other way once again. So, the powerful man in charge does something terrible and gets away with it. I guess you have learned something from mortals after all.

ZEUS: They do seem to love that, don't they?

HERA: But we'll all be keeping an eye on you, dear. After all, we have nothing better to do under quarantine. Very well, everyone, crisis averted go back to...whatever you're all doing.

(Grumbles and eye-rolls as all the other participants windows close, leaving only Zeus.)

ZEUS: *(To the audience:)* And just what are you looking at? Yes, you won today. But if this kind of pandemic thing ever happens again...you had better *hope* I don't have a lightning bolt with your name on it.

(Zeus points to the viewers as his window closes.)

(End of play.)

The Author Speaks

What inspired you to write this play?

It was spring of 2020, and COVID-19 was raging everywhere. Schools were shut down and everyone was canceling their stage productions. So, like every other playwright, I was scrambling to write something that could be performed via video conference. At first I was writing just monologues, but I quickly realized that it would be more exciting to have people interacting in one-on-one Zoom chats. My own kids are obsessed with superheroes and Greek mythology, and I had been working on some more straightforward adaptations of myths, so the idea of having all-powerful beings dealing with the same problems of quarantine that we were seemed like a lot of fun.

Was the structure or other elements of the play influenced by any other work?

I suppose structurally it's a bit like ***La Ronde***, with a series of two-character scenes where one character carries over into the next, and it eventually comes full-circle. For the mythology, I was definitely influenced by Rick Riordan's work. My kids introduced me to *Percy Jackson*, and I really admire the way he has used myths and updated the characters for the 21st century. One thing I was watchful of was making sure I didn't make my versions of the gods too similar to his—"Well, his Poseidon is kind of a beach bum, so I should make mine more like a rich Connecticut guy with a yacht," and so on.

Have you dealt with the same theme in other works that you have written?

Before I wrote this, I wrote ***Super Heroes Under Quarantine***, which is published by Brooklyn Publishers. It's the same structure and a somewhat similar mystery plot with pastiche versions of Marvel and DC characters. I was considering doing more, like maybe a Disney parody called ***The Happiest Place on Earth Under Quarantine*** or a *Star Wars* one called ***Quarantined in a Galaxy Far Far Away,*** but I think I'm moving on. I have done some work adapting Greek myths for the stage before, and it's very fun to find the heart of those stories and make them relevant for modern audiences, and to figure out how to deal with the more gory or salacious plot elements.

What writers have had the most profound effect on your style?
I'm a great admirer of classic Broadway, so George S. Kaufman and his many collaborators—Marc Connelly, Edna Ferber, Moss Hart and others—are major influences, as are the greats who followed in their footsteps like Neil Simon, Christopher Durang and Larry Shue. And, of course, as an 80s kid, I was very influenced by TV—from the classic comedy rhythms on *Sesame Street* to, of course, Monty Python and *The Simpsons* and *Saturday Night Live*. My kids have been discovering my old comic strip collections lately, and it's been reminding me how much I learned from reading Charles Schulz, Garry Trudeau, Bill Watterson, Gary Larson and Bill Amend.

What do you hope to achieve with this work?
For now, I hope it will allow schools and theatres that can't stage traditional plays a chance to have fun putting on a show. When things get back to normal after we're all vaccinated (fingers crossed), I think Zoom theatre will still be a part of life, so I hope this play will continue to get produced past 2021—maybe as an artifact of that weird year we all lived through, but, I hope, as a vital, enjoyable piece of theatre. And I hope someday it will get staged live, with an audience, because nothing beats seeing real living, breathing people reacting to a story being told right in front of them.

What were the biggest challenges involved in the writing of this play?

One challenge was figuring out how to incorporate as many characters from mythology as possible. Something I learned from parodying *Harry Potter* and Marvel and *Star Wars* is that every character is somebody's favorite, and if you don't include a version of even a minor character, people will miss it. Plus, I wanted the play to have at least as many female characters as male, because, invariably, more girls than boys show up to audition for school plays. Luckily, and perhaps sadly, Greek mythology, as macho as it is, actually probably has a better gender balance than a lot of modern pop culture. But I wasn't worried about having too large a cast, because this play naturally lends itself to double-casting. I think you could stage this with three or four actors, which would be incredibly fun. Then, once I had all the characters, figuring out how to work them into the natural flow of the story, and making sure everyone had a job to do was tricky but invigorating.

What are the most common mistakes that occur in productions of your work?

I try not to get too bothered about "mistakes," because my plays are usually staged by schools and the performers are all learning and growing from the experience. That said, sure they make mistakes. Modern kids didn't grow up with as much exposure to older popular culture as Generation X and the Boomers did, so they don't necessarily have as innate an understanding of the rhythms and standards of comedy as those of us who watched older movies and shows did. And it's hard for young actors to understand the difference between playing a character broadly but a moment naturally. You can be silly and sincere at the same time, but it's hard to find the balance. And, while I love it when productions add their own bits or moments to my plays, sometimes they'll stick in something that works well enough on its own but winds up fighting against or undermining the original script—though much more often these new additions enhance the experience.

What inspired you to become a playwright?
I grew up in a theatrical family—my father and my uncle were both actors who appeared in a lot of local plays. I did quite a bit of acting as a kid, and when I got to high school, we did an annual student-written play festival, so I started writing plays for that. Now, for some reason, my high school managed to turn out a lot of playwrights. In 2014 the three finalists for the Pulitzer Prize in Drama were Annie Baker, who graduated from Amherst Regional High School a few years after me, and Madeleine George, who graduated from ARHS a few years before me, and Lisa Kron, who didn't go to my high school, but is married to Madeleine. So apparently I was in a good environment to foster playwrights. In college I wanted to do it all—write, act, direct, everything. But I quickly learned that a lot of my classmates were much better at the acting and directing than I was, so I focused on the writing, and I have been ever since.

How did you research the subject?
I had been reading up on Greek myths for another project anyway, but primarily I relied on help from two nine-year-old experts who lived with me. My twins were in fourth grade, and they loved Greek myths and especially Rick Riordan's take on them. Their school has a year-long unit on Greek myths for fourth graders, and one of the last public things I got to do before we all started social distancing was to see a class play based on Theseus and the Minotaur where one of my sons played the minotaur, in the same costume he had worn for the previous Halloween.

Are any characters modeled after real life or historical figures?
I had great fun borrowing from modern characters and people to capture the right voices for these ancient gods. So Hera has a bit of Jessica Walter from *Arrested Development* about her. Dionysus is reminiscent of Jon Lovitz's Master Thespian character. Hephaestus is based on the two hosts of NPR's *Car Talk*. Apollo has a bit of Keanu Reeves as Ted about him. Poseidon is a bit of Jim Backus from *Gilligan's Island,* along with a million other comic rich guys. Hestia is inspired by Martha Stewart. I hear Patrick Warburton in my head when I read Hercules's lines. And Demeter isn't based on someone specific but sort of a general type of woman I saw a lot of, growing up in Amherst (MA) at the farmer's market.

What is your writing process?
It depends on the project. For this one, I did a lot of plotting on a white board to figure out which character would call which other character and why and what that conversation would lead to next. I wrote this while I was also semi-supervising my kids' remote schooling in the spring of 2020. Luckily, my twins were old enough to navigate the day without much guidance, but my kindergartner needed a bit more assistance, and my preschooler needed a lot of help filling his day. Still, I managed to be very productive amidst all of that, which is not always the case for me. I would never wish another pandemic on the world, but I did appreciate the time it gave me to write.

Shakespeare gave advice to the players in *Hamlet;* if you could give advice to your cast what would it be?
Hey! Dionysus actually paraphrases that speech in this play when he says Hermes is speaking too trippingly on the tongue.

My advice—Have lots of fun with this. Make big, big choices. But remember that as broad as your characters are, they are still part of a story, and you must keep in mind your part in the story and how you help to move it along and how you contribute to the comedy. Even in a play as silly as this, the characters have needs and desires, and they are making choices and taking action to get what they want. Be clear, consistent and in-the-moment, and it will help the comedy and the story.

How was the first production different from the vision that you created in your mind?

It was pretty spot-on, actually. Very solid performances from a young cast. I was intrigued that they went with fairly classical-looking costumes—togas and armor and such. I guess I was thinking they might have used modern dress—maybe I was thinking about how Rick Riordan's gods are always in suits and leather jackets and stuff. They had amazing-looking backgrounds, which I really loved and surprised me a bit—these were actual printed backdrops the actors put up behind themselves, not Zoom trickery.

Is there anything else you'd like to tell us?

The first draft of this play was a bit more PG-13, with jokes about how often marital infidelity plays into myths, jokes about how the gods sometimes married their own siblings and procreated with them, and the original version of Dionysus was all about his nature as god of wine, with his portrayal as more of a boozy W.C. Fields type. These jokes wouldn't really fly with our intended demographic of middle schools and high schools, so I cut them out. I'm always a little sad to cut a joke I like, but I have to remind myself that they're just words, and the play is better off this way.

About the Author

Dean O'Carroll is a playwright and parodist originally from Amherst, Massachusetts. His parody plays ***Back to the 80s: A Risky, Goonie, Breakfasty Tale of Totally Tubular Time Travel; Star Stars: The Franchise Awakens; Marvelous Squad: A Super-Heroic Tale with Avengeance; The Humor Games*** and the ***Sally Cotter*** trilogy are published by Playscripts and have been staged by schools and theatres around the world. His online play ***Choose Your Heist*** is published by Heuer Publishing. Dean has also written material for "Weekend Update" on *Saturday Night Live* and several children's books about DC Comics superheroes. Dean holds a BA in Drama from Vassar College and an MFA in Playwriting from Brandeis University. He has taught writing at Quinnipiac University, Simmons College, CUNY, Occidental College and Widener University. He lives outside Philadelphia with his wife and their four children.

About YouthPLAYS

YouthPLAYS (www.youthplays.com) is a publisher of award-winning professional dramatists and talented new discoveries, each with an original theatrical voice, and all dedicated to expanding the vocabulary of theatre for young actors and audiences. On our website you'll find one-act and full-length plays and musicals for teen and pre-teen (and even college) actors, as well as duets and monologues for competition. Many of our authors' works have been widely produced at high schools and middle schools, youth theatres and other TYA companies, both amateur and professional, as well as at elementary schools, camps, churches and other institutions serving young audiences and/or actors worldwide. Most are intended for performance by young people, while some are intended for adult actors performing for young audiences.

YouthPLAYS was co-founded by professional playwrights Jonathan Dorf and Ed Shockley. It began merely as an additional outlet to market their own works, which included a substantial body of award-winning published and unpublished plays and musicals. Those interested in their published plays were directed to the respective publishers' websites, and unpublished plays were made available in electronic form. But when they saw the desperate need for material for young actors and audiences—coupled with their experience that numerous quality plays for young people weren't finding a home—they made the decision to represent the work of other playwrights as well. Dozens and dozens of authors are now members of the YouthPLAYS family, with scripts available both electronically and in traditional acting editions. We continue to grow as we look for exciting and challenging plays and musicals for young actors and audiences.

About ProduceaPlay.com

Let's put up a play! Great idea! But producing a play takes time, energy and knowledge. While finding the necessary time and energy is up to you, ProduceaPlay.com is a website designed to assist you with that third element: knowledge.

Created by YouthPLAYS' co-founders, Jonathan Dorf and Ed Shockley, ProduceaPlay.com serves as a resource for producers at all levels as it addresses the many facets of production. As Dorf and Shockley speak from their years of experience (as playwrights, producers, directors and more), they are joined by a group of award-winning theatre professionals and experienced teachers from the world of academic theatre, all making their expertise available for free in the hope of helping this and future generations of producers, whether it's at the school or university level, or in community or professional theatres.

The site is organized into a series of major topics, each of which has its own page that delves into the subject in detail, offering suggestions and links for further information. For example, Publicity covers everything from Publicizing Auditions to How to Use Social Media to Posters to whether it's worth hiring a publicist. Casting details Where to Find the Actors, How to Evaluate a Resume, Callbacks and even Dealing with Problem Actors. You'll find guidance on your Production Timeline, The Theater Space, Picking a Play, Budget, Contracts, Rehearsing the Play, The Program, House Management, Backstage, and many other important subjects.

The site is constantly under construction, so visit often for the latest insights on play producing, and let it help make your play production dreams a reality.

More from YouthPLAYS

Many Maids Made Me Murder (or maybe the butler did do it) by Kemuel DeMoville
Comedy. 55-65 minutes. 15-45+ any gender.

The butler did it. Maids know this to be true, and years ago, they banded together into the Sacred Order of Maids to dispense "Maid justice" against butlers gone rogue. Now they gather once more —this time via video—to right the wrongs, but with the sudden passing of their entire leadership, did the butlers do it again, or are they in need of their own deep cleaning from within? Hilarity and lots of wacky wordplay ensue in this murder-mystery written for virtual performance.

Me, My Selfie & I by Jonathan Dorf
Dramedy. 40-50 minutes (flexible). 2-20 females, 2-20+ males (6-40+ performers possible).

We live in a world of social media, one in which we seem to be recording our every experience. But are we making memories or missing out on them? Through a series of scenes and monologues—everything from an accidental first date to a most unusual art exhibit to creating that last, best selfie—we meet a group of teens who are struggling to find the balance between documenting their lives and living them.

Hero Zero by Lojo Simon
Dramedy. 20-25 minutes. 2 females, 2 males, 7 any gender.

Big Bro is a war hero, a larger-than-life presence whose little brother wants to be just like him when he grows up. But when the unthinkable happens and Big Bro is lost in the war, how can young Nil fill such big shoes? There are no easy answers, but Big Bro may just have left some clues behind to help in this play about grief and resilience, written for virtual performance.

Goddess of Tears by Keegon Schuett
Drama. 80-90 minutes. 8 females, 3 males, 4+ any gender.

Since nearly the beginning of time, Niobe has served as the Goddess of Tears in the digital Cloud of Olympus, approving or denying access to every single teardrop. But with mortal requests reaching staggering proportions and a memory pecking at her, it may be time for her to quit the program...if only the other gods would let her. Alone, Niobe searches for a connection that's stronger than the divine wi-fi. Will she finally find herself again after all these years and tears, or will she be disconnected for all of eternity? Written for virtual performance.

Sleepy Hollow by Elizabeth Doyle (music), Judy Freed (book), Owen Kalt (lyrics)
Musical Comedy. 90 minutes (may be cut down to a 60-minute version). 5+ females, 6+ males (11+ performers possible).

A scheming schoolmaster. An apprehensive heiress. A restless ghost with a penchant for decapitation. And a teenage girl who thinks demons are delightful. Nothing is as it seems in this fresh, funny adaptation of Washington Irving's classic American tale, *The Legend of Sleepy Hollow*.

Nana's Happy Happy Good News Only Video Chat by Hillary DePiano
Comedy. 30-40 minutes. 7-10 any gender.

What do you do when it's Nana's birthday and a storm ruins your big bash? If you're her grandkids, you take the party virtual with a birthday video chat! The one rule: No bad news to ruin Nana's special day—no matter what. But can this group of disasters make it look like they've got their act together, or will life have other plans?

Made in the USA
Middletown, DE
02 April 2021